AFRICAN AMERICAN ANSWER BOOK

# ARTS AND ENTERTAINMENT

# CHELSEA HOUSE PUBLISHERS

# AFRICAN AMERICAN ANSWER BOOK

## Available in Hardcover • 6 Titles

| | | |
|---|---|---|
| ❒ | Arts and Entertainment (0–7910–3201-9) | $12.95 |
| ❒ | Biography (0–7910–3203–5) | $12.95 |
| ❒ | Facts and Trivia (0–7910–3211–6) | $12.95 |
| ❒ | History (0–7910–3209–4) | $12.95 |
| ❒ | Science and Discovery (0–7910–3207–8) | $12.95 |
| ❒ | Sports (0–7910–3205-1) | $12.95 |

## Available in Paperback • 6 Titles

| | | |
|---|---|---|
| ❒ | Arts and Entertainment (0–7910–3202-7) | $3.95 |
| ❒ | Biography (0–7910–3204–3) | $3.95 |
| ❒ | Facts and Trivia (0–7910–3212–4) | $3.95 |
| ❒ | History (0–7910–3210–8) | $3.95 |
| ❒ | Science and Discovery (0–7910–3208–6) | $3.95 |
| ❒ | Sports (0–7910–3206–X) | $3.95 |

**Mail to**: Chelsea House Publishers, Dept. Mail Order, P.O. Box 914, 1974 Sproul Road, Suite 400, Broomall, PA 19008-0914

Please send me the book(s) I have checked above.

My payment of $_____ is enclosed. (Please add $1.00 per order to cover postage and handling. PA residents add 6% sales tax.)

Method of payment: ❒ Cash  ❒ Check  ❒ Money Order
    ❒ Discover  ❒ VISA  ❒ MasterCard

Credit Card Number: _____

Expiration Date: _____

Phone Number: _____

Signature: _____

Please allow 6 weeks for delivery.

Name _____

Address _____

City _____ State _____ Zip _____

AFRICAN AMERICAN ANSWER BOOK

# ARTS AND ENTERTAINMENT

## 325 QUESTIONS DRAWN FROM THE EXPERTISE OF HARVARD'S DU BOIS INSTITUTE

R. S. Rennert

Chelsea House Publishers
New York   Philadelphia

**CHELSEA HOUSE PUBLISHERS**
*EDITORIAL DIRECTOR* Richard Rennert
*EXECUTIVE MANAGING EDITOR* Karyn Gullen Browne
*COPY CHIEF* Robin James
*PICTURE EDITOR* Adrian G. Allen
*ART DIRECTOR* Robert Mitchell
*MANUFACTURING DIRECTOR* Gerald Levine
*ASSISTANT ART DIRECTOR* Joan Ferrigno

**AFRICAN AMERICAN ANSWER BOOK**
*SERIES ORIGINATOR AND ADVISER* Ken Butkus
*ASSISTANT EDITOR* Annie McDonnell
*DESIGNER* John Infantino
*PICTURE RESEARCHER* Sandy Jones

3   5   7   9   8   6   4   2

Rennert, Richard Scott, 1956-
   African American answer book, arts and entertain-
ment: 325 questions drawn from the expertise of
Harvard's Du Bois Institute / R.S. Rennert.
   p. cm.
   Includes Index
ISBN 0-7910-3201-9
       0-7910-3202-7 (pbk.)
   1. Afro-American arts-Miscellanea-Juvenile litera-
ture. 2.Afro-American artists-Miscellanea-Juvenile
literature. [1.Entertainers-Miscellanea.  2. Afro-
Americans-Miscellanea. 3. Questions and answers.]  I.
Title
NX512.3.A35R46  1995                    94-29999
700' .89'96073-dc20                          CIP
                                              AC

**PICTURE CREDITS**
Archive Photos: p. 23; Archive Photos/Frank Driggs
Collection: p. 26; The Bettmann Archive: p. 46; Schom-
berg Center for Research in Black Culture, Astor, Lenox
& Tilden Foundations, New York Public Library: pp. 40,
50; Springer/Bettmann Film Archive: p. 34; UPI/Bet-
tmann: pp. 10, 15, 18, 31.

# CONTENTS

# INTRODUCTION

In creating the BLACK AMERICANS OF ACHIEVEMENT series for Chelsea House Publishers, I was fortunate enough to work closely with Nathan Irvin Huggins, one of America's leading scholars in the field of black studies and director of the W. E. B. Du Bois Institute for Afro-American Research at Harvard University. His innumerable contributions to the books have not only helped to make BLACK AMERICANS OF ACHIEVEMENT an award-winning series, but his expressed commitment to inform readers about the rich heritage and accomplishments of African Americans has encouraged Chelsea House to draw from his work and develop the 325 questions that make up this *African American Answer Book.*

Each of these briskly challenging questions has been designed to stimulate thought and discussion about African American history. The answers highlight either the leading figures of black America or focus on previously unsung yet equally inspiring African American heroes, their achievements, and their legacies.

You can use these questions to test your own knowledge or to stump your friends. Either way, you will find that this *African American Answer Book*—like its companion volumes—is bound to educate as well as entertain.

—R. S. R.

# QUESTIONS

**1.** What 1987 play, written by Alfred Unry, became a movie in 1989?

    **a** - *The Color Purple*
    **b** - *Driving Miss Daisy*
    **c** - *Porgy and Bess*

**2.** Who was the star of the 1977 movie *The Greatest?*

    **a** - *Muhammad Ali*
    **b** - *Joe Frazier*
    **c** - *George Foreman*

**3.** Who wrote *The Autobiography of Malcolm X?*

    **a** - *Alex Haley*
    **b** - *Amiri Baraka*
    **c** - *Alice Walker*

**4.** What play was written by Lorraine Hansberry?

    **a** - *Driving Miss Daisy*
    **b** - *A Raisin in the Sun*
    **c** - *The Wiz*

**5.** Who is known as the "Queen of Soul"?

    **a** - *Ella Fitzgerald*
    **b** - *Lena Horne*
    **c** - *Aretha Franklin*

**6.** Whose well-known songs include "Ain't That a Shame," "I'm Walkin'," and "Poor Me"?

    **a** - *Fats Domino*
    **b** - *David Ruffin*
    **c** - *Teddy Pendergrass*

**7.** For what profession is Leona Mitchell known?

    **a** - *Dancer*
    **b** - *Opera singer*
    **c** - *Actress*

**8.** Who directed the movie *Boyz N the Hood?*

    **a** - *Spike Lee*
    **b** - *John Singleton*
    **c** - *Bill Cosby*

**9.** Who was the first African American poet to be nationally recognized for his writing?

    **a** - *James Baldwin*
    **b** - *Langston Hughes*
    **c** - *Paul Laurence Dunbar*

**10.** Who was the first African American woman to win an Academy Award?

    **a** - *Hattie McDaniel*
    **b** - *Whoopi Goldberg*
    **c** - *Cicely Tyson*

**11.** Who wrote the famous song "Say it Loud, I'm Black and I'm Proud"?

    **a** - *James Brown*
    **b** - *Nat "King" Cole*
    **c** - *Sammy Davis, Jr.*

**12.** The book *Roots* was made into a movie in what year?

    **a** - *1969*
    **b** - *1977*
    **c** - *1982*

**13.** Who began his career as the drummer for Harold Melvin and the Blue Notes and went on to become a popular solo artist?

    **a** - *Teddy Pendergrass*
    **b** - *Luther Vandross*
    **c** - *David Ruffin*

**14.** Who directed the movie *She's Gotta Have It?*

  **a** - *Samella Sanders Lewis*
  **b** - *Spike Lee*
  **c** - *Amiri Baraka*

**15.** In 1986, Dexter Gordon was nominated for an Oscar for his performance in what film?

  **a** - *'Round Midnight*
  **b** - *Purple Rain*
  **c** - *The Color Purple*

**16.** B.B. King is noted for what type of music?

  **a** - *Rock*
  **b** - *Blues*
  **c** - *Country*

**17.** Eartha Kitt played what role in the Batman TV series?

  **a** - *Cat Woman*
  **b** - *Batgirl*
  **c** - *Aunt Harriet*

**18.** In what year was the movie *Off to Bloomingdale Asylum* released?

  **a** - *1902*
  **b** - *1926*
  **c** - *1946*

**19.** (True or False) Chuck D. and Flavor Flav are the lead singers of the Gap Band.

**20.** Who is known as one of the greatest African American jazz piano players?

  **a** - *Charlie Parker*
  **b** - *Duke Ellington*
  **c** - *John Coltrane*

**21.** Keenen Ivory Wayans is the producer of what TV comedy show?

  **a** - *"Saturday Night Live"*
  **b** - *"In Living Color "*
  **c** - *"The Cosby Show"*

*Marian Anderson, who has been called "the voice of the American soul," defied prejudice to attain international renown, becoming the first black singer to perform with the Metropolitan Opera.*

**22.** What famous singer played guitar for Little Richard before starting his solo career?

      **a** - *Ronald Isley*
      **b** - *Jimi Hendrix*
      **c** - *James Brown*

**23.** In what movie did Prince have a starring role?

      **a** - *Purple Rain*
      **b** - *Roots*
      **c** - *Boyz N the Hood*

**24.** Sidney Poitier became the first African American to win the Best Actor Oscar for his starring role in what film?

    **a** - *To Sir with Love*
    **b** - *Lilies of the Field*
    **c** - *Guess Who's Coming to Dinner*

**25.** What group was comprised of Diana Ross, Florence Ballard, and Mary Wilson?

    **a** - *The Supremes*
    **b** - *The Vandellas*
    **c** - *The Chiffons*

**26.** What was Louis Armstrong's nickname?

    **a** - *Jazzie*
    **b** - *Trumpy*
    **c** - *Satchmo*

**27.** What producer/songwriter originated New Jack Swing?

    **a** - *Teddy Riley*
    **b** - *Spike Lee*
    **c** - *Amiri Baraka*

**28.** What record company did Berry Gordy, Jr., create?

    **a** - *RCA*
    **b** - *Motown*
    **c** - *Arista*

**29.** The movie *Buck and the Preacher* was directed by what famous African American actor?

    **a** - *Bill Cosby*
    **b** - *Sidney Poitier*
    **c** - *Harry Belafonte*

**30.** Who was the star of the film *Raw?*

    **a** - *Eddie Murphy*
    **b** - *Bill Cosby*
    **c** - *Keenen Ivory Wayans*

**31.** What is the name of Alice Walker's Pulitzer Prize–winning novel?

    **a** - *Driving Miss Daisy*
    **b** - *The Color Purple*
    **c** - *Roots*

**32.** Billie Holiday's life was the subject of what famous film?

    **a** - *Mahogany*
    **b** - *Lady Sings the Blues*
    **c** - *The Color Purple*

**33.** (True or False) Lena Horne began her career performing at the Cotton Club in New York City.

**34.** Who appeared with Richard Widmark in *Death of a Gunfighter?*

    **a** - *Lena Horne*
    **b** - *Phylicia Rashad*
    **c** - *Lisa Bonet*

**35.** Who became Hollywood's first black millionaire?

    **a** - *Bill "Bojangles" Robinson*
    **b** - *Bill Cosby*
    **c** - *Stepin Fetchit*

**36.** Why did Paul Robeson go to England to make several films?

    **a** - *Hollywood filmmakers felt white America would not pay to see black movie stars*
    **b** - *Hollywood wanted to produce films in England*
    **c** - *He enjoyed producing foreign movies*

**37.** (True or False) Phillis Wheatley was purchased as a slave by Susannah Wheatley, a 52-year-old Christian woman.

**38.** Phillis Wheatley came to the U.S. from West Africa at age seven or eight. How long did it take her to understand the English language?

    **a** - *8 months*
    **b** - *16 months*
    **c** - *2 years*

**39.** What was the name of the character played by Bill Cosby in "The Cosby Show"?

    **a** - *Dr. Cliff Huxtable*
    **b** - *Fat Albert*
    **c** - *Chet Kincaid*

**40.** What prime-time show featuring Bill Cosby was canceled after six weeks?

    **a** - *"The New Bill Cosby Show"*
    **b** - *"COS"*
    **c** - *"The Electric Company"*

**41.** What company has a successful series of television commercials that started in 1974 and features Bill Cosby?

    **a** - *Dutch Masters*
    **b** - *Jell-O pudding*
    **c** - *Kodak*

**42.** What African American female comic was known as "Moms"?

    **a** - *Jackie Mabley*
    **b** - *Florence Mills*
    **c** - *Josephine Baker*

**43.** Who was the first African American to win an Oscar for Best Actor?

    **a** - *Sidney Poitier*
    **b** - *Nat "King" Cole*
    **c** - *Bill Robinson*

**44.** Who portrayed Scarlett O'Hara's mammy in the 1939 film *Gone with the Wind*?

    **a** - *Ethel Waters*
    **b** - *Josephine Baker*
    **c** - *Hattie McDaniel*

**45.** Who was Charles Chesnutt?

    **a** - *America's first published black novelist*
    **b** - *America's first  recognized black actor*
    **c** - *Newspaper reporter*

**46.** What was Charles Chesnutt's final novel?

    **a** - *The Quarry*
    **b** - *The Marked Tree*
    **c** - *Concerning Father*

**47.** (True or False) Charles Chesnutt was the author of *Uncle Tom's Cabin.*

**48.** *Uncle Tom's Cabin* was published in what year?

    **a** - *1845*
    **b** - *1852*
    **c** - *1858*

**49.** Of the following, who was not a black poet?

    **a** - *Langston Hughes*
    **b** - *Countee Cullen*
    **c** - *Eubie Blake*

**50.** The Roaring Twenties introduced an unprecedented outpouring of black art, literature, and music. What was this period known as?

    **a** - *New Age*
    **b** - *Harlem Renaissance*
    **c** - *Victorian Period*

**51.** What African American took jazz vocals to a new level and was called "The Divine One" because of her range and effortless mastery of the intricacies of music?

    **a** - *Sarah Vaughan*
    **b** - *Marian Anderson*
    **c** - *Leontyne Price*

**52.** Who has become one of the most celebrated authors of our time, addressing the issues of race and women's rights?

    **a** - *Alice Walker*
    **b** - *Jane Cooper*
    **c** - *Nella Larsen*

**53.** What jazz singer was born Eleanora Fagan in 1915?

    **a** - *Ella Fitzgerald*
    **b** - *Lena Horne*
    **c** - *Billie Holiday*

*A multitalented artist with a keen social awareness, Maya Angelou has inspired multitudes with her unforgettable autobiographies and her stirring poetry.*

**54.** (True or False) *Cotton Comes to Harlem* was written by James Baldwin.

**55.** What famous black author said, "Black writers must do more than merely exhibit rage, they must analyze the roots of racial oppression"?

    **a** - *James Weldon Johnson*
    **b** - *Ralph Ellison*
    **c** - *James Baldwin*

**56.** (True or False) James Baldwin is the author of *Notes of a Native Son.*

**57.** Arturo Toscanini's remark, "Yours is a voice one hears once in a hundred years," referred to what singer?

    **a** - *Ella Fitzgerald*
    **b** - *Marian Anderson*
    **c** - *Lena Horne*

**58.** What dictator secretly attended one of Marian Anderson's performances?

    **a** - *Adolf Hitler*
    **b** - *Joseph Stalin*
    **c** - *Benito Mussolini*

**59.** (True or False) Rudolf Bing invited Marian Anderson to sing at the Metropolitan Opera.

**60.** Who was known as "The Lady from Philadelphia"?

    **a** - *Marian Anderson*
    **b** - *Billie Holiday*
    **c** - *Josephine Baker*

**61.** (True or False) W. C. Handy assembled and managed Louis Armstrong and the All Stars.

**62.** (True or False) Zutty Singleton was a jazz drummer who played with The Hot Five.

**63.** In 1925, Louis Armstrong and Bessie Smith collaborated on how many instant hits?

    **a** - *3*
    **b** - *5*
    **c** - *10*

**64.** What is the name of Debbie Allen's sister, who appeared on "The Cosby Show"?

    **a**- *Phylicia Rashad*
    **b**- *Lisa Bonet*
    **c**- *Cicely Tyson*

**65.** Maya Angelou is best known as a:

    **a** - *Singer and dancer*
    **b** - *Writer and poet*
    **c** - *Musician and composer*

**66.** Who authored the book *Roots?*

    **a** - *Langston Hughes*
    **b** - *Alice Walker*
    **c** - *Alex Haley*

**67.** What poet and playwright was named LeRoi Jones?

   **a** - *Amiri Baraka*
   **b** - *Spike Lee*
   **c** - *Langston Hughes*

**68.** Who wrote *Narrative of the Life of Frederick Douglass?*

   **a** - *James Baldwin*
   **b** - *Frederick Douglass*
   **c** - *Langston Hughes*

**69.** What famous serial autobiography was written by Maya Angelou?

   **a** - *I Know Why the Caged Bird Sings*
   **b** - *The Color Purple*
   **c** - *You Can't Keep a Good Woman Down*

**70.** Who is the author of *The Color Purple?*

   **a** - *Alice Walker*
   **b** - *Maya Angelou*
   **c** - *Toni Morrison*

**71.** Which of the following books was a Pulitzer Prize–winner for Toni Morrison?

   **a** - *Beloved*
   **b** - *The Temple of My Familiar*
   **c** - *The Third Life of Grange Copeland*

**72.** Who wrote *Their Eyes Were Watching God?*

   **a** - *Zora Neale Hurston*
   **b** - *Alice Walker*
   **c** - *Louise Meriwether*

**73.** Who is best known for her role as Bloody Mary in the 1949 Broadway stage production of *South Pacific?*

   **a** - *Diahann Carroll*
   **b** - *Juanita Hall*
   **c** - *Ruby Dee*

**74.** Who was the first African American woman to have her own weekly television series, "Julia"?

   **a** - *Tina Turner*
   **b** - *Diana Ross*
   **c** - *Diahann Carroll*

*One of America's most beloved entertainers, Louis Armstrong revolutionized jazz and helped establish it as the nation's first highly popular black art form.*

**75.** What famous singer launched her career with the Supremes?

> **a** - *Diana Ross*
> **b** - *Lena Horne*
> **c** - *Dionne Warwick*

**76.** (True or False) Dionne Warwick made "Why Do Fools Fall in Love?" a hit song.

**77.** What was Ira Aldridge's profession?

> **a** - *Dancer*
> **b** - *Singer*
> **c** - *Actor*

**78.** Who was the first African American to achieve fame as a sculptress?

> **a** - *Harriet Tubman*
> **b** - *Edmonia Lewis*
> **c** - *Sojourner Truth*

**79.** In what state was Langston Hughes born?

    **a** - *Missouri*
    **b** - *New York*
    **c** - *Illinois*

**80.** A. Clayton Bates overcame what handicap to become a legendary dancer?

    **a** - *Loss of eyesight*
    **b** - *Loss of hearing*
    **c** - *Loss of left leg*

**81.** Who was the author of *Uncle Tom's Cabin?*

    **a** - *Harriet Beecher Stowe*
    **b** - *Alice Walker*
    **c** - *Langston Hughes*

**82.** How old was Langston Hughes when his poetry was first published?

    **a** - *12*
    **b** - *19*
    **c** - *25*

**83.** (True or False) Cab Calloway was one of the top nightclub performers and big band leaders during the 1930s.

**84.** What 1989 movie won several Academy Awards, including Best Picture?

    **a** - *The Color Purple*
    **b** - *Driving Miss Daisy*
    **c** - *Porgy and Bess*

**85.** Who assisted Duke Ellington with his composing and arranging?

    **a** - *Billy Strayhorn*
    **b** - *Count Basie*
    **c** - *Cab Calloway*

**86.** Elizabeth Taylor Greenfield was one of the best known soprano singers in the 1850s and was referred to as the:

    **a** - *Guiding Voice*
    **b** - *Black Swan*
    **c** - *Black Soul*

**87.** Jacob Lawrence chronicled the life of African Americans through his:

    **a** - *Artistic paintings*
    **b** - *Novels*
    **c** - *Poetry*

**88.** Who played the role of Bill Cosby's son on "The Cosby Show"?

    **a** - *Denzel Washington*
    **b** - *Malcolm Jamal Warner*
    **c** - *James Earl Jones*

**89.** Wynton Marsalis is a famous African American:

    **a** - *Singer*
    **b** - *Actor*
    **c** - *Musician*

**90.** Stephen Bentley scored syndication success with his cartoon strip:

    **a** - *Herb and Jamaal*
    **b** - *Jump Start*
    **c** - *Calvin and Hobbes*

**91.** In what year did the cartoon strip Herb and Jamaal debut?

    **a** - *1988*
    **b** - *1989*
    **c** - *1990*

**92.** Robb Armstrong is the creator of what cartoon strip, which features the trials and tribulations of Joe and Marcy?

    **a** - *Herb and Jamaal*
    **b** - *For Better or for Worse*
    **c** - *Jump Start*

**93.** Name the Grammy Award–winning Philadelphia quartet that sold over 4 million copies of their album *Cooley High Harmony.*

    **a** - *Boyz II Men*
    **b** - *Kris Kross*
    **c** - *Take 6*

**94.** Who won a Tony Award for his performance in the Broadway musical *Jelly's Last Jam?*

    **a** - *Laurence Fishburne*
    **b** - *Gregory Hines*
    **c** - *James Earl Jones*

**95.** Who is the author of the critically acclaimed novel *Waiting To Exhale?*

    **a** - *Alice Walker*
    **b** - *Zora Neale Hurston*
    **c** - *Terry McMillan*

**96.** Who is the award-winning singer who recorded the platinum album called *The Comfort Zone?*

    **a** - *Vanessa Williams*
    **b** - *Tina Turner*
    **c** - *Whitney Houston*

**97.** What artist recorded the songs "I Will Always Love You," "The Greatest Love of All," and "I Wanna Dance with Somebody"?

    **a** - *Mariah Carey*
    **b** - *Whitney Houston*
    **c** - *Regina Belle*

**98.** What is the name of Ray Billingsley's comic strip which traces the ups and downs of a black youth growing up in the inner city?

    **a** - *Wee Pals*
    **b** - *Where I'm Coming From*
    **c** - *Curtis*

**99.** Brumsic Brandon, Jr., is best known for what comic strip?

    **a** - *Luther*
    **b** - *Quincy*
    **c** - *Scruples*

**100.** Who sold more than 20 million albums and collected more than 700,000 pounds of food for charity during the 1992 "Too Legit To Quit" tour?

    **a** - *Speech*
    **b** - *M.C. Hammer*
    **c** - *Michael Jackson*

**101.** Actress Nichelle Nichols is best known for her role in what television series?

    **a** - *"The Bill Cosby Show"*
    **b** - *"A Different World"*
    **c** - *"Star Trek "*

**102.** What African American cartoonist created the world famous "Wee Pals"?

    **a** - *Morrie Turner*
    **b** - *Ray Billingsley*
    **c** - *Stephen Bentley*

**103.** What modern-day African American model is regarded as one of the hottest runway and print models?

    **a** - *Sara Lou Harris*
    **b** - *Naomi Campbell*
    **c** - *Borthea Towles*

**104.** Who is the founder of the Dance Theater of Harlem?

    **a** - *Katherine Dunham*
    **b** - *Alvin Ailey*
    **c** - *Arthur Mitchell*

**105.** Who is regarded as the first African American journalist?

    **a** - *Mal Goode*
    **b** - *John Russwurm*
    **c** - *Frederick Douglass*

**106.** What African American is a daytime TV star on "All My Children" and also appeared in "Dynasty," "Poltergeist," and "Streets of Fire"?

    **a** - *Nathan Purdee*
    **b** - *Richard Lawson*
    **c** - *Richard Biggs*

**107.** What acclaimed dancer/choreographer blended African and Caribbean rhythms into modern dance?

    **a** - *Judith Jamison*
    **b** - *Janet Collins*
    **c** - *Katherine Dunham*

*Bill Cosby rose from a childhood of absolute poverty to become America's favorite humorist. An Emmy Award–winning actor and best-selling author, he has also earned a doctorate in education.*

**108.** What black actress won an Academy Award for her supporting role in the movie *Ghost?*

    **a** - *Whoopi Goldberg*
    **b** - *Robin Givens*
    **c** - *Cicely Tyson*

**109.** What was the name of the music/dance television show hosted by Marilyn McCoo?

    **a** - *"Soul Train"*
    **b** - *"Solid Gold "*
    **c** - *"American Bandstand"*

**110.** Who is the host of "Soul Train"?

    **a** - *Marilyn McCoo*
    **b** - *Arsenio Hall*
    **c** - *Don Cornelius*

**111.** Who wrote *The Escape,* the first published play by an African American?

    **a** - *William Wells Brown*
    **b** - *Frederick Douglass*
    **c** - *Phillis Wheatley*

**112.** What famous narrative was written by Solomon Northrup, a fugitive slave?

    **a** - *My Bondage & My Freedom*
    **b** - *Narrative of a Slave*
    **c** - *A Narrative of Slave Life in the U.S.*

**113.** Who was born in Florence, Alabama, in 1873 and is called "Father of the Blues"?

    **a** - *Scott Joplin*
    **b** - *W. C. Handy*
    **c** - *Louis Armstrong*

**114.** What actress, featured in the hit television series "Head of the Class," was once briefly married to boxer Mike Tyson?

    **a** - *Halle Berry*
    **b** - *Jasmine Guy*
    **c** - *Robin Givens*

**115.** Where was the birthplace of bandleader and composer Duke Ellington?

    **a** - *New York*
    **b** - *Chicago*
    **c** - *Washington, D.C.*

**116.** In what city was Louis Armstrong born?

    **a** - *Chicago*
    **b** - *New Orleans*
    **c** - *New York*

**117.** What was the name of the first novel published by Charles W. Chesnutt?

    **a** - *The Colonel's Dream*
    **b** - *Native Son*
    **c** - *The House Behind the Cedars*

**118.** Countee Cullen was a distinguished poet who achieved fame during what decade?

    **a** - *1920s*
    **b** - *1950s*
    **c** - *1970s*

**119.** (True or False) In 1903, W. E. B. Du Bois published *Souls of Black Folk.*

**120.** (True or False) The first blues composition published by W. C. Handy was called "Memphis Blues."

**121.** What Richard Wright book was one of the best-sellers of 1940?

    **a** - *The House Behind the Cedars*
    **b** - *Native Son*
    **c** - *Uncle Tom's Cabin*

**122.** Dizzy Gillespie and Charlie Parker were innovators of what type of music in the early 1940s?

    **a** - *Blues*
    **b** - *Dixie*
    **c** - *Bebop*

**123.** What famous musician ran for president of the United States?

    **a** - *Dizzy Gillespie*
    **b** - *Duke Ellington*
    **c** - *Scott Joplin*

**124.** What famous musician's trademark was puffing cheeks and a trumpet bell that pointed skyward?

    **a** - *Louis Armstrong*
    **b** - *Dizzy Gillespie*
    **c** - *Palmer Davis*

**125.** Who delighted millions with tunes like "Groovin' High," "Manteca," "Salt Peanuts," and "Con Alma"?

    **a** - *Louis Armstrong*
    **b** - *Charlie Parker*
    **c** - *Dizzy Gillespie*

*One of the most respected figures in the history of American music, Duke Ellington used his talents as both a bandleader and a composer to elevate jazz into a serious art form.*

**126.** In a matter of months, I went from running an elevator to being the most famous young poet in America. Who am I?

    **a** - *Paul Laurence Dunbar*
    **b** - *James Baldwin*
    **c** - *Langston Hughes*

**127.** Who won an Oscar for his role in the 1989 film *Glory?*

    **a** - *James Earl Jones*
    **b** - *Denzel Washington*
    **c** - *Louis Gossett, Jr.*

**128.** What was the name of the first published novel written by an African American [William Wells Brown]?

    **a** - *The Black Man*
    **b** - *The Negro in the American Rebellions*
    **c** - *Clotel; or, the President's Daughter*

**129.** (True or False) Maya Angelou was the first African American woman to have an original screenplay produced.

**130.** What was the name of the first screenplay produced by an African American woman?

    **a** - *Georgia, Georgia*
    **b** - *Driving Miss Daisy*
    **c** - *A Raisin in the Sun*

**131.** What is the name of the record label started by Berry Gordy, Jr.?

    **a** - *Arista*
    **b** - *Motown*
    **c** - *Epic*

**132.** What was the amount of the first royalty check that Berry Gordy, Jr., received?

    **a** - *$340.00*
    **b** - *$34.00*
    **c** - *$3.40*

**133.** What is the music-related nickname of Detroit?

    **a** - *Motown*
    **b** - *Kool City*
    **c** - *Soul City*

**134.** The Four Tops, the Temptations, Martha and the Vandellas, and Mary Wells came from what major city?

    **a** - *New York*
    **b** - *Detroit*
    **c** - *Philadelphia*

**135.** Who wrote the song "Darling Nelly Gray," which was published in 1856 and brought attention to the human toll of slavery?

    **a** - *Scott Joplin*
    **b** - *Alexander Pushkin*
    **c** - *Benjamin Hanby*

**136.** Who was the author of the hit play *A Raisin in the Sun?*

    **a** - *Lorraine Hansberry*
    **b** - *Alice Walker*
    **c** - *Virginia Hamilton*

**137.** Who was the first black to win a Pulitzer Prize?

    **a** - *Charles Chesnutt*
    **b** - *Gwendolyn Brooks*
    **c** - *Langston Hughes*

**138.** What is the name of the Pulitzer Prize–winning book of poetry written by Gwendolyn Brooks?

    **a** - *A Street in Bronzeville*
    **b** - *In the Mecca*
    **c** - *Annie Allen*

**139.** Who was the first black star of his own TV variety show?

    **a** - *Nat "King" Cole*
    **b** - *Flip Wilson*
    **c** - *Bill Cosby*

**140.** What was the name of the first successful TV variety show starring an African American?

    **a** - *"The Bill Cosby Show"*
    **b** - *"The Nat King Cole Show "*
    **c** - *"The Flip Wilson Show"*

**141.** "The Nat King Cole Show" ran for 64 weeks from 1956–1957 and was sponsored by:

    **a** - *A greeting card company*
    **b** - *A cigarette company*
    **c** - *A hair tonic company*

**142.** What profession is shared by Al Roker, Mark McEwen, and Spencer Christian?

    **a** - *Sportscaster*
    **b** - *Anchorman*
    **c** - *Weatherman*

**143.** What was the name of James Baldwin's 1963 best-seller, which electrified both black and white Americans?

    **a** - *The Fire Next Time*
    **b** - *Go Tell It on the Mountain*
    **c** - *Another Country*

**144.** Who portrayed "Ulrica" in *The Masked Ball,* was named to the U.S. Delegation to the United Nations, and was awarded the Freedom Medal?

    **a** - *Lena Horne*
    **b** - *Marian Anderson*
    **c** - *Josephine Baker*

**145.** Who starred in the movie *The Watermelon Man?*

    **a** - *Sidney Poitier*
    **b** - *Godfrey Cambridge*
    **c** - *Louis Gossett, Jr.*

**146.** Who sang the theme song for the hit TV series "Moonlighting"?

    **a** - *Al Jarreau*
    **b** - *Peabo Bryson*
    **c** - *George Benson*

**147.** Who founded the magazine *Ebony?*

    **a** - *Earl G. Graves*
    **b** - *John H. Johnson*
    **c** - *Esther Jackson*

**148.** What title was inspired by a Langston Hughes poem?

    **a** - *Driving Miss Daisy*
    **b** - *A Raisin in the Sun*
    **c** - *The Color Purple*

**149.** Who was the first black woman to own a TV studio?

    **a** - *Debbie Allen*
    **b** - *Oprah Winfrey*
    **c** - *Cicely Tyson*

**150.** Who starred in the blockbuster movie *Beverly Hills Cop?*

    **a** - *Danny Glover*
    **b** - *Eddie Murphy*
    **c** - *Denzel Washington*

**151.** What was the name of the movie that was based on the life of Steven Biko, a South African freedom fighter?

    **a** - *Home of the Brave*
    **b** - *Cry Freedom*
    **c** - *Lilies of the Field*

**152.** Who was the black star of the TV series "I Spy"?

    **a** - *Richard Pryor*
    **b** - *Bill Cosby*
    **c** - *Cleavon Little*

**153.** Who was the first African American to appear on the cover of *Vogue* magazine?

    **a** - *Vanessa Williams*
    **b** - *Beverly Johnson*
    **c** - *Naomi Sims*

**154.** What was the real name of comedian Redd Foxx?

    **a** - *John Elroy Foxx*
    **b** - *John Elroy Sanford*
    **c** - *John Redrick Foxx*

**155.** What is Little Richard's real name?

    **a** - *Richard Pennington*
    **b** - *Richard Lewis*
    **c** - *Richard Hampton*

**156.** Who was the first African American artist to win national recognition?

    **a** - *Romare Bearden*
    **b** - *Robert Scott Duncanson*
    **c** - *Aaron Douglas*

**157.** (True or False) The movie *Jo Jo Dancer, Your Life Is Calling* is based on the life of Sidney Poitier.

**158.** What was the nickname of renowned jazz musician Charlie Parker?

    **a** - *Bird*
    **b** - *Jazzie*
    **c** - *Chas*

**159.** Who wrote the famous book about lynching called *The Red Record?*

    **a** - *Ida B. Wells-Barnett*
    **b** - *Charles Chesnutt*
    **c** - *Langston Hughes*

*Ella Fitzgerald has been widely hailed as "the First Lady of Jazz." She is best known for her musical range and her distinctive scat singing, which established her as a top vocalist.*

**160.** What African American was acclaimed for his involvement in the design of the Philadelphia Museum of Art?

    **a** - *Julian Abele*
    **b** - *Max Bond*
    **c** - *Paul Williams*

**161.** What was the nickname of jazz saxophonist Coleman Hawkins?

    **a** - *Bean*
    **b** - *Jazzie*
    **c** - *Sax*

**162.** Who was the leader of the King Oliver Creole Jazz Band?

    **a** - *Louis Armstrong*
    **b** - *Joseph Oliver*
    **c** - *Count Basie*

**163.** Who starred in the movie *A Woman Called Moses?*

    **a** - *Cicely Tyson*
    **b** - *Nichelle Nichols*
    **c** - *Debbie Allen*

**164.** (True or False) Nikki Giovanni is a famous African American poet.

**165.** What is Hammer's real name?

    **a** - *Stanley Kirk Burrell*
    **b** - *M. C. Harris*
    **c** - *James Hammer*

**166.** What actor played the role of Charlie "Bird" Parker in the 1988 movie *Bird?*

    **a** - *Forest Whitaker*
    **b** - *Louis Gossett, Jr.*
    **c** - *James Earl Jones*

**167.** "Ma" Rainey was known as the:

    **a** - *Mother of the Blues*
    **b** - *Mother of Soul*
    **c** - *Mother of Rap*

**168.** Who was the first African American woman to be recognized as an award-winning composer?

    **a** - *Florence Price*
    **b** - *Shirley DuBois*
    **c** - *Philippa Schuyler*

**169.** Who was the first African American dancer to become a member of a classical ballet company?

    **a** - *Bill "Bojangles" Robinson*
    **b** - *Arthur Mitchell*
    **c** - *Katherine Dunham*

**170.** Who was the first African American woman to have a full-length novel published?

    **a** - *Frances Ellen Watkins Harper*
    **b** - *Zora Neale Hurston*
    **c** - *Alice Walker*

**171.** Who was the first African American to become famous for his work as a symphonic conductor?

    **a** - *James DePriest*
    **b** - *Dean Dixon*
    **c** - *Henry Lewis*

**172.** Who played the role of "Dwayne Wayne" on the TV series "A Different World"?

    **a** - *Kadeem Hardison*
    **b** - *Malcolm Jamal Warner*
    **c** - *Denzel Washington*

**173.** What African American singer won the *Esquire* New Star Award in 1946?

    **a** - *Billy Eckstine*
    **b** - *Nat King Cole*
    **c** - *Louis Armstrong*

**174.** In what year did Quincy Jones win five Grammy Awards?

    **a** - *1983*
    **b** - *1988*
    **c** - *1992*

**175.** Who played the role of the Scarecrow in the movie version of *The Wiz?*

    **a** - *Michael Jackson*
    **b** - *Danny Glover*
    **c** - *Malcolm Jamal Warner*

**176.** Who was the first African American singer to be admitted to the Metropolitan Opera Company in New York City?

    **a** - *Marian Anderson*
    **b** - *Ella Fitzgerald*
    **c** - *Mahalia Jackson*

**177.** (True or False) Louis Armstrong is known as the "King of Ragtime."

**178.** Who was the leader of the first African American band to play in Carnegie Hall?

    **a** - *Count Basie*
    **b** - *Louis Armstrong*
    **c** - *Duke Ellington*

**179.** What African American author was awarded the Pulitzer Prize for fiction in 1988?

    **a** - *Toni Morrison*
    **b** - *Alice Walker*
    **c** - *Alex Haley*

*An influential leader of the Harlem Renaissance, Langston Hughes infused his poems and plays with rhythms from black spirituals and jazz to eloquently voice his race's hopes and struggles.*

**180.** Who wrote the song "Maple Leaf Rag"?

    **a** - *Scott Joplin*
    **b** - *Louis Armstrong*
    **c** - *Duke Ellington*

**181.** What song was the first hit for Gladys Knight and the Pips?

    **a** - *"I Heard It Through the Grapevine"*
    **b** - *"Every Beat of My Heart"*
    **c** - *"Midnight Train to Georgia"*

**182.** By what other name is jazz musician Fritz Jones known?

    **a** - *Ahmad Jamal*
    **b** - *Malcolm Jones*
    **c** - *Frederick Brooks*

**183.** Robert Hooks and Douglas Turner Ward founded what theater group in New York City?

    **a** - *Association of Black Artists*
    **b** - *Negro Ensemble Company*
    **c** - *Negro Fellowship League*

**184.** Who was the first African American actor to receive featured billing in a movie?

    **a** - *Stepin Fetchit*
    **b** - *Sidney Poitier*
    **c** - *Paul Robeson*

**185.** What African American jazz musician, in 1950, was the first to give a solo recital in the United States?

    **a** - *Scott Joplin*
    **b** - *Erroll Garner*
    **c** - *W. C. Handy*

**186.** What is the name of the black painter who is known for his African American murals?

    **a** - *Norma Morgan*
    **b** - *Aaron Douglas*
    **c** - *Ernest Crichlow*

**187.** What African American actress had a role in the movie *A Raisin in the Sun?*

    **a** - *Cicely Tyson*
    **b** - *Oprah Winfrey*
    **c** - *Diana Sands*

**188.** *Appeal,* a book of anti-slavery literature, was written by what African American?

    **a** - *David Walker*
    **b** - *Frederick Douglass*
    **c** - *Langston Hughes*

**189.** Who is regarded as the finest African American woman painter?

    **a** - *Lois Jones Pierre-Noel*
    **b** - *Elizabeth Catlett*
    **c** - *Norma Morgan*

**190.** What is the name of the Marion Marche Perkins sculpture that won the Art Institute of Chicago Purchase Award in 1951?

    **a** - *Freedom*
    **b** - *Man of Sorrow*
    **c** - *Life as a Slave*

**191.** Who was the female lead singer of the Fifth Dimension?

    **a** - *Marilyn McCoo*
    **b** - *Diana Ross*
    **c** - *Tina Turner*

**192.** Name the singer whose nickname is "Little Moses."

    **a** - *Eddie Floyd*
    **b** - *Isaac Hayes*
    **c** - *Otis Redding*

**193.** Who wrote a play with Zora Neale Hurston?

    **a** - *Langston Hughes*
    **b** - *Chester Himes*
    **c** - *LeRoi Jones*

**194.** What was Duke Ellington's given name?

    **a** - *Edward Kennedy Ellington*
    **b** - *Joseph Michael Ellington*
    **c** - *Steven John Ellington*

**195.** In what year did the first Broadway play written by an African American woman open in New York City?

    **a** - *1955*
    **b** - *1959*
    **c** - *1962*

**196.** Who is called "the Queen of the Blues"?

    **a** - *Billie Holiday*
    **b** - *Dinah Washington*
    **c** - *Lena Horne*

**197.** Who is regarded as "the King of Tap Dancers"?

    **a** - *Bill "Bojangles" Robinson*
    **b** - *Sammy Davis, Jr.*
    **c** - *Stepin Fetchit*

**198.** (True or False) Ray Charles is the Honorary Life Chairman of the Rhythm and Blues Hall of Fame.

**199.** Who earned the nickname "Mr. Bojangles"?

    **a** - *Dizzy Gillespie*
    **b** - *Bill Robinson*
    **c** - *Charlie Parker*

**200.** Who taught Louis Armstrong how to play the trumpet?

    **a** - *Dizzy Gillespie*
    **b** - *Joseph "King" Oliver*
    **c** - *Willis "Ray" Nance*

**201.** Who is known as America's unofficial "Ambassador of Jazz"?

    **a** - *Scott Joplin*
    **b** - *Billy Taylor*
    **c** - *Louis Armstrong*

**202.** What composer used African American motifs in his music?

    **a** - *Beethoven*
    **b** - *Chopin*
    **c** - *Sousa*

**203.** What is Clerow Wilson's stage name?

    **a** - *Wade Wilson*
    **b** - *Flip Wilson*
    **c** - *Ollie Wilson*

**204.** Who rose to the top of the Rhythm and Blues charts in 1964?

    **a** - *Dionne Warwick*
    **b** - *Ella Fitzgerald*
    **c** - *Marian Anderson*

**205.** Who was the saxophonist in Bruce Springsteen's former rock group the E Street Band?

    **a** - *Vince Andrews*
    **b** - *Grover Washington, Jr.*
    **c** - *Clarence Clemons*

**206.** Who is the publisher of the monthly magazine *Black Enterprise?*

    **a** - *John Johnson*
    **b** - *Samuel Cornish*
    **c** - *Earl Graves*

**207.** (True or False) In 1969, Bill Cosby's NBC television program was called "The Bill Cosby Show."

**208.** (True or False) Mahalia Jackson earned the title "Queen of the Gospel Song."

**209.** (True or False) Berry Gordy, Jr., founded the Arista Record Corporation in 1959.

**210.** What was Chubby Checker's longest-running hit song on the Top 40 Charts?

    **a** - *"The Twist"*
    **b** - *"The Pony"*
    **c** - *"Heard It Through the Grapevine"*

**211.** For how many weeks did the hit song "The Twist" stay on the Top 40 charts?

    **a** - *12*
    **b** - *33*
    **c** - *50*

**212.** Who made his living in the early 1800s as a portrait painter?

    **a** - *Romare Bearden*
    **b** - *Mark Jones*
    **c** - *Joshua Johnston*

**213.** Howard Rollins received an Oscar nomination for what movie?

    **a** - *Lilies of the Field*
    **b** - *Home of the Brave*
    **c** - *Ragtime*

**214.** What famous African American author/poet read at President Bill Clinton's inauguration in 1993?

    **a** - *Amiri Baraka*
    **b** - *Phillis Wheatley*
    **c** - *Maya Angelou*

**215.** Charles Alston was recognized for his outstanding career as a sculptor, painter, and:

  **a** - *Singer*
  **b** - *Dancer*
  **c** - *Teacher*

**216.** Danny Glover is recognized as an accomplished:

  **a** - *Musician*
  **b** - *Actor*
  **c** - *Painter*

**217.** Who acted in *Home of the Brave, The Sandpiper,* and *The Caine Mutiny?*

  **a** - *Paul Winfield*
  **b** - *Frederick O'Neal*
  **c** - *James Edwards*

**218.** Al Jarreau is an accomplished:

  **a** - *Singer*
  **b** - *Actor*
  **c** - *Dancer*

**219.** Beauford Delaney liked to paint what subjects?

  **a** - *Black writers and artists*
  **b** - *Civil War casualties*
  **c** - *Slaves*

**220.** Beauford Delaney's paintings can be found on display in what New York City museum?

  **a** - *Whitney Museum*
  **b** - *Metropolitan Museum of Art*
  **c** - *Museum of Modern Art*

**221.** *The Guinness Book of World Records* lists what Michael Jackson album as the best-selling of all time?

  **a** - *Thriller*
  **b** - *Man in the Mirror*
  **c** - *Bad*

*Writing in one of the most distinctive voices in American literature, novelist and folklorist Zora Neale Hurston brought to life the people she called "the Negroes furthest down."*

**222.** Who made the stainless steel sculpture of two wing-like shapes framed by neon lights at the entrance to the Miami International Airport?

    **a** - *Elizabeth Catlett*
    **b** - *Frederick Eversley*
    **c** - *Paul Keene*

**223.** Vanessa Bell appeared on what soap opera?

    **a** - *"General Hospital"*
    **b** - *"The Guiding Light"*
    **c** - *"All My Children"*

**224.** Mary Leontyne Price is famous for being:

    **a** - *An opera singer*
    **b** - *A jazz musician*
    **c** - *A blues singer*

**225.** Who was the disc jockey and entertainer who wrote several famous dance songs, including "The Funky Chicken," "The Funky Penguin," and "The Dog"?

    **a** - *Rufus Thomas*
    **b** - *Don Cornelius*
    **c** - *Marilyn McCoo*

**226.** What musical instrument did Nat "King" Cole play?

    **a** - *Saxophone*
    **b** - *Trumpet*
    **c** - *Piano*

**227.** Who is musical director of the Royal Ballet of London, and a music director and conductor of the Dayton, Ohio, Philharmonic Orchestra?

    **a** - *Isaiah Jackson*
    **b** - *John Coltrane*
    **c** - *Maya Angelou*

**228.** What dancer became interested in the African roots of dance while studying anthropology at the University of Chicago?

    **a** - *Gregory Hines*
    **b** - *Sammy Davis, Jr.*
    **c** - *Katherine Dunham*

**229.** Who wrote *Clotel; or, the President's Daughter,* the first published novel by an African American, in 1853?

    **a** - *William Wells Brown*
    **b** - *Richard Wright*
    **c** - *Langston Hughes*

**230.** What musical instrument does jazz musician Grover Washington, Jr., play?

    **a** - *Trombone*
    **b** - *Clarinet*
    **c** - *Saxophone*

**231.** Who was the first black network television anchor?

    **a** - *Max Robinson*
    **b** - *Bryant Gumbel*
    **c** - *Bernard Shaw*

**232.** Who was the first African American musician to perform concert tours?

    **a** - *Dizzy Gillespie*
    **b** - *Joseph Douglass*
    **c** - *Louis Armstrong*

**233.** Elizabeth Catlett is best recognized as a:

    **a** - *Sculptress*
    **b** - *Author*
    **c** - *Singer*

**234.** Who was the first African American master of ceremonies of a nationally televised show?

    **a** - *Bill Cosby*
    **b** - *Flip Wilson*
    **c** - *Nipsey Russell*

**235.** What actor appeared in the play *Emperor Jones* in 1925?

    **a** - *Oscar Micheaux*
    **b** - *Frederick O'Neal*
    **c** - *Paul Robeson*

**236.** In 1921, Edward (Kid) Ory recorded *Ory's Creole Trombone and Society Blues,* the first known recordings by an African American of what type of music?

    **a** - *Ragtime*
    **b** - *Jazz*
    **c** - *Gospel*

**237.** The Cotton Club was a famous:

    **a** - *Nightclub*
    **b** - *Opera House*
    **c** - *Theater*

**238.** In what year did poet Sterling Brown die?

    **a** - *1940*
    **b** - *1960*
    **c** - *1990*

**239.** (True or False) James Brown is referred to as "The Father of Soul."

**240.** (True or False) Hazel Scott appeared and sang in the hit film *Home of the Brave.*

**241.** Julian Abele was involved in the design of what museum?

    **a** - *Smithsonian Institution*
    **b** - *The Museum of Modern Art*
    **c** - *Philadelphia Museum of Art*

**242.** Who starred in the box office hit *Trading Places?*

    **a** - *Eddie Murphy*
    **b** - *Richard Pryor*
    **c** - *Bill Cosby*

**243.** What role did Jester Hairston play on the TV sitcom "Amen"?

    **a** - *Minister*
    **b** - *Deacon*
    **c** - *Choir Leader*

**244.** Johnny Mathis is famous for singing what type of songs?

    **a** - *Gospel*
    **b** - *Ballads*
    **c** - *Soul*

**245.** Who was Laura Wheeler Waring?

    **a** - *Musician*
    **b** - *Painter*
    **c** - *Dancer*

**246.** "Ma" Rainey taught what singer how to sing the blues?

    **a** - *Marian Anderson*
    **b** - *Ella Fitzgerald*
    **c** - *Bessie Smith*

**247.** What is the surname of entertainers La Toya, Janet, and Michael?

    **a** - *Johnson*
    **b** - *Cosby*
    **c** - *Jackson*

**248.** (True or False) Bill Cosby's first best-selling book was entitled *Fatherhood.*

**249.** In 1966, Leontyne Price opened the Metropolitan Opera season as what character?

    **a** - *Clarissa Dalloway*
    **b** - *Cleopatra*
    **c** - *Emma Bovary*

**250.** In 1954, Joe Williams sang with whose band?

    **a** - *Duke Ellington's*
    **b** - *Louis Armstrong's*
    **c** - *Count Basie's*

**251.** What actor now warns others of the dangers of drug abuse, after his own near-death experience?

    **a** - *Bill Cosby*
    **b** - *Eddie Murphy*
    **c** - *Richard Pryor*

**252.** Who wrote *Uncle Tom's Children?*

    **a** - *Richard Wright*
    **b** - *Langston Hughes*
    **c** - *Alice Walker*

**253.** Ida B. Wells-Barnett was the author of *The Red Book,* the first :

    **a** - *African American novel*
    **b** - *Authentic record of lynchings*
    **c** - *Authentic record of black history*

**254.** Where was Ralph Waldo Ellison, the famous African American novelist, born?

    **a** - *Philadelphia, Pennsylvania*
    **b** - *Nashville, Tennessee*
    **c** - *Oklahoma City, Oklahoma*

**255.** What African American novelist wrote *Invisible Man,* for which he won the National Book Award for fiction in 1952?

    **a** - *Ralph Ellison*
    **b** - *Richard Wright*
    **c** - *Chester Himes*

**256.** Who wrote a number one best-seller that became a 12-hour TV miniseries?

   **a** - *Alex Haley*
   **b** - *Maya Angelou*
   **c** - *Alice Walker*

**257.** What was the book *Uncle Tom's Cabin* about?

   **a** - *Recorded black lynchings*
   **b** - *Characterized plight of slaves*
   **c** - *Recognized African American achievements*

**258.** Nat Love wrote what kind of stories?

   **a** - *Mysteries*
   **b** - *Science Fiction*
   **c** - *Westerns*

**259.** Who wrote "A Negro Love Song"?

   **a** - *Langston Hughes*
   **b** - *Paul Laurence Dunbar*
   **c** - *Chester Himes*

**260.** Who wrote *The Lost Zoo,* a classic children's book?

   **a** - *Maya Angelou*
   **b** - *Countee Cullen*
   **c** - *Alice Walker*

**261.** Amiri Baraka (a.k.a. LeRoi Jones) authored:

   **a** - *The Color Purple*
   **b** - *Roots*
   **c** - *Blues People*

**262.** *Blues People* is about:

   **a** - *African American music*
   **b** - *African American politicians*
   **c** - *African American authors*

**263.** George Washington commended what African American woman for her literary achievements?

   **a** - *Sojourner Truth*
   **b** - *Zora Neale Hurston*
   **c** - *Phillis Wheatley*

*A gifted composer, Scott Joplin strongly contributed to the gain in national prominence that ragtime music, a predecessor of jazz, achieved in the early 1900s.*

**264.** (True or False) Langston Hughes wrote *Before the Mayflower.*

**265.** Who is the author of *Black Metropolis,* written in 1945?

    **a** - *Horace Clayton*
    **b** - *Richard Wright*
    **c** - *Zora Neale Hurston*

**266.** In what year did the poet Paul Laurence Dunbar die?

    **a** - *1880*
    **b** - *1906*
    **c** - *1946*

**267.** For what talent did Elizabeth Taylor Greenfield receive worldwide acclaim?

    **a** - *Singer with a range of 27 octaves*
    **b** - *Dancer with over 27 styles*
    **c** - *Musician who played 8 instruments*

**268.** Who was one of the first African American stars of the silver screen?

    **a** - *Ethel Waters*
    **b** - *Nina Mae McKinney*
    **c** - *Pam Grier*

**269.** What musical instrument used in Africa was frequently chosen as a royal or sacred instrument?

    **a** - *Xylophone*
    **b** - *Tambourine*
    **c** - *Drum*

**270.** "Balafou," an African term, refers to what?

    **a** - *Drum*
    **b** - *Xylophone*
    **c** - *Fiddle*

**271.** In 1905, the first black symphony was founded. What was it called?

    **a** - *Boston Symphony*
    **b** - *Cleveland Concert Symphony*
    **c** - *Philadelphia Concert Orchestra*

**272.** In 1899, "The Maple Leaf Rag" was composed by:

    **a** - *W. C. Handy*
    **b** - *Scott Joplin*
    **c** - *"Jelly Roll" Morton*

**273.** What was the name of the first publication of a jazz arrangement?

    **a** - *"Maple Leaf Rag"*
    **b** - *"Memphis Blues"*
    **c** - *"Jelly Roll Blues"*

**274.** Who was "Big Jim" Simpson?

    **a** - *A tuba player*
    **b** - *A Hollywood stuntman*
    **c** - *A fiddle-playing cowboy*

**275.** What electric guitar player was regarded as the "King of Chicago Blues"?

    **a** - *B. B. King*
    **b** - *Muddy Waters*
    **c** - *W. C. Handy*

**276.** Who was known as the "Godfather of Disco-Soul" and made "You Are the Sunshine of My Life" a hit song?

    **a** - *James Brown*
    **b** - *Ray Charles*
    **c** - *Stevie Wonder*

**277.** Who played the character "Denise" in "The Cosby Show"?

    **a** - *Keshia Knight Pulliam*
    **b** - *Tempestt Bledsoe*
    **c** - *Lisa Bonet*

**278.** What pop-rock star has devoted much of his life and music to his belief that "children are our future"?

    **a** - *Luther Vandross*
    **b** - *Stevie Wonder*
    **c** - *Michael Jackson*

**279.** What black artist achieved world fame with his painted biblical scenes?

    **a** - *Meta Fuller*
    **b** - *Henry Tanner*
    **c** - *Romare Bearden*

**280.** Who was regarded as a master guitar player and developed a program for learning the guitar?

    **a** - *Justin Holland*
    **b** - *Sylvester Weaver*
    **c** - *"Papa" Charlie Jackson*

**281.** What blueswoman recorded the hit songs "Down Hearted Blues" and "Gulf Coast Blues"?

    **a** - *Clara Smith*
    **b** - *Bessie Smith*
    **c** - *Victoria Spivey*

**282.** Florence Price was world renowned for her:

    **a** - *Award-winning music compositions*
    **b** - *Theatrical performances*
    **c** - *Paintings and sculptures*

**283.** Who wrote *The African Origin of Civilization* in 1969?

    **a** - *Peter Bergman*
    **b** - *Anta Cheikh Diop*
    **c** - *Donald Henderson*

**284.** Who is the author of *The Destruction of Black Civilization?*

    **a** - *Benjamin Quarles*
    **b** - *Chancellor Williams*
    **c** - *Ivan Van Sertima*

**285.** Who played "Fiddler" in the TV miniseries *Roots?*

    **a** - *James Earl Jones*
    **b** - *Louis Gossett, Jr.*
    **c** - *Alex Haley*

**286.** Who wrote the book *Born To Rebel?*

    **a** - *Lerone Bennett, Jr.*
    **b** - *Paul Laurence Dunbar*
    **c** - *Benjamin E. Mays*

**287.** Who wrote *What Manner of Man,* a biography of Martin Luther King, Jr.?

    **a** - *Alex Haley*
    **b** - *Alice Walker*
    **c** - *Lerone Bennett, Jr.*

**288.** What is the name of the book written by Benjamin Quarles?

    **a** - *From Slavery to Freedom*
    **b** - *The Black Abolitionists*
    **c** - *Roots*

**289.** What is the name of the famous children's book written by Countee Cullen?

    **a** - *Mother Goose*
    **b** - *The Lost Zoo*
    **c** - *Little Angel*

**290.** *To Be or Not to Bop* is about:

    **a** - *Black music*
    **b** - *Slavery*
    **c** - *Black nationalism*

*Addressing the issues of race and women's rights with the spirit of a literary heroine, Alice Walker has become one of the most celebrated authors of our time.*

**291.** The Creole Jazz Band was led by:

    **a** - *Louis Armstrong*
    **b** - *Duke Ellington*
    **c** - *Joseph "King" Oliver*

**292.** What was Ferdinand Morton's nickname?

    **a** - *Bo Diddley*
    **b** - *Fats*
    **c** - *Jelly Roll*

**293.** Benny Golson wrote scores for what television show?

    **a** - *"The Six Million Dollar Man"*
    **b** - *"It Takes a Thief"*
    **c** - *"Mission Impossible "*

**294.** Quincy Jones wrote a full-length score for what Hollywood movie?

    **a** - *Cheech and Chong's Next Movie*
    **b** - *The Godfather*
    **c** - *In Cold Blood*

**295.** For what style of music were the Ward Singers famous?

    **a** - *Pop-Gospel*
    **b** - *Soul*
    **c** - *Rhythm and Blues*

**296.** "Bentwa" was a musical instrument unique to Africa. What kind of instrument was it?

    **a** - *Drum*
    **b** - *Musical bow*
    **c** - *Xylophone*

**297.** What musical group has released albums entitled *Funky Divas, Remix To Sing,* and *Born To Sing?*

    **a** - *Heavy D and The Boyz*
    **b** - *The Temptations*
    **c** - *En Vogue*

**298.** (True or False) Robert L. Johnson started Black Entertainment Television.

**299.** What musical artist released the hit album *Power of Love?*

    **a** - *Freddie Jackson*
    **b** - *Luther Vandross*
    **c** - *Lionel Richie*

**300.** Who played "Mr. T" in the TV series "The A-Team"?

    **a** - *Lawrence Tayrue*
    **b** - *Denzel Washington*
    **c** - *Roger Mosely*

**301.** Robert Guillaume starred in what TV series?

    **a** - *"A Different World"*
    **b** - *"The Jeffersons"*
    **c** - *"Benson"*

**302.** Who starred in the TV series "The Jeffersons"?

    **a** - *Redd Foxx*
    **b** - *Bill Cosby*
    **c** - *Sherman Hemsley*

**303.** Who was the first African American to win the Nobel Prize in Literature?

    **a** - *Toni Morrison*
    **b** - *James Baldwin*
    **c** - *Alice Walker*

**304.** Sherman Hemsley starred in what two TV series?

    **a** - *"The Jeffersons" and "Amen"*
    **b** - *"Good Times" and "Sanford and Son"*
    **c** - *"Good Times" and "The A-Team"*

**305.** Ed Bradley is a member of what news team?

    **a** - *"20/20"*
    **b** - *"Prime Time Live"*
    **c** - *"60 Minutes"*

**306.** On the TV series "Magnum, P.I." what was Roger Mosely's nickname?

    **a** - *Mr. T*
    **b** - *T. C.*
    **c** - *Sammie*

**307.** Who starred in the TV sitcom "Different Strokes"?

    **a** - *Gary Coleman*
    **b** - *Redd Foxx*
    **c** - *Sherman Hemsley*

**308.** In what TV series was a character named "Buck-wheat" one of the stars?

    **a** - *"Amos N' Andy"*
    **b** - *"The Little Rascals "*
    **c** - *"The Cosby Kids"*

**309.** Who was a sidekick on "The Jack Benny Show"?

    **a** - *Stepin Fetchit*
    **b** - *Flip Wilson*
    **c** - *Eddie "Rochester" Anderson*

**310.** In 1969, President Richard Nixon awarded the Presidential Medal of Freedom to:

    **a** - *Dizzy Gillespie*
    **b** - *Duke Ellington*
    **c** - *Stevie Wonder*

**311.** (True or False) Phillis Wheatley was the first African American to win a Pulitzer Prize.

**312.** Who wrote the book *Annie Allen* in 1949?

  **a** - *Gwendolyn Brooks*
  **b** - *Phillis Wheatley*
  **c** - *Amiri Baraka*

**313.** (True or False) Scott Joplin was awarded the Pulitzer Prize after his death.

**314.** What artist's painting is entitled *After Church?*

  **a** - *Gordon Parks*
  **b** - *Gwendolyn Brooks*
  **c** - *Romare Bearden*

**315.** Who was the composer of "Take the 'A' Train"?

  **a** - *Billy Strayhorn*
  **b** - *Scott Joplin*
  **c** - *Ray Charles*

**316.** (True or False) Oscar Micheaux directed *Birthright,* the first full-length black film.

**317.** What novelist wrote *The Fire Next Time* during the freedom movement of the 1960s?

  **a** - *Langston Hughes*
  **b** - *Zora Neale Hurston*
  **c** - *James Baldwin*

**318.** Who was the most popular poet in the mid- to late 1800s?

  **a** - *Countee Cullen*
  **b** - *Frances Harper*
  **c** - *Langston Hughes*

**319.** What actress starred in the movie *Sounder?*

  **a** - *Cicely Tyson*
  **b** - *Hattie McDaniel*
  **c** - *Whoopi Goldberg*

**320.** Who received a special award from the Academy of Motion Picture Arts and Sciences for his "Uncle Remus" role in the Walt Disney production *Song of the South?*

  **a** - *James Edwards*
  **b** - *Paul Robeson*
  **c** - *James Baskett*

**321.** (True or False) James Edwards portrayed a black soldier in the 1949 movie *Home of the Brave*.

**322.** In what movie did Sidney Poitier make his screen debut?

    **a** - *Edge of the City*
    **b** - *The Defiant Ones*
    **c** - *No Way Out*

**323.** Who was the first African American woman director (*Georgia, Georgia,* 1972)?

    **a** - *Whoopi Goldberg*
    **b** - *Oprah Winfrey*
    **c** - *Maya Angelou*

**324.** What filmmaker produced and directed *Do the Right Thing, Jungle Fever,* and *Malcolm X?*

    **a** - *Robert Townsend*
    **b** - *John Singleton*
    **c** - *Spike Lee*

**325.** Who starred in the movie *The Bodyguard?*

    **a** - *Vanessa Williams*
    **b** - *Whitney Houston*
    **c** - *Cicely Tyson*

# ANSWERS

1. b *Driving Miss Daisy*
2. a Muhammad Ali
3. a Alex Haley
4. b *A Raisin in the Sun*
5. c Aretha Franklin
6. a Fats Domino
7. b Opera singer
8. b John Singleton
9. c Paul Laurence Dunbar
10. a Hattie McDaniel
11. a James Brown
12. b 1977
13. a Teddy Pendergrass
14. b Spike Lee
15. a *'Round Midnight*
16. b Blues
17. a Cat Woman
18. a 1902
19. False - Public Enemy
20. b Duke Ellington
21. b "In Living Color"
22. b Jimi Hendrix
23. a *Purple Rain*
24. b *Lilies of the Field*
25. a The Supremes
26. c Satchmo
27. a Teddy Riley
28. b Motown
29. b Sidney Poitier
30. a Eddie Murphy
31. b *The Color Purple*
32. b *Lady Sings the Blues*
33. True
34. a Lena Horne
35. c Stepin Fetchit
36. a Hollywood filmmakers felt white America
    would not pay to see black movie stars
37. True

38. b **16 months**
39. a **Dr. Cliff Huxtable**
40. b **"COS"**
41. b **Jell-O pudding**
42. a **Jackie Mabley**
43. a **Sidney Poitier**
44. c **Hattie McDaniel**
45. a **America's first published black novelist**
46. a ***The Quarry***
47. **False - Harriet Beecher Stowe**
48. b **1852**
49. c **Eubie Blake**
50. b **Harlem Renaissance**
51. a **Sarah Vaughan**
52. a **Alice Walker**
53. c **Billie Holiday**
54. **False - Chester Himes**
55. c **James Baldwin**
56. **True**
57. b **Marian Anderson**
58. b **Joseph Stalin**
59. **True**
60. a **Marian Anderson**
61. **False - Joe Glaser**
62. **True**
63. b **5**
64. a **Phylicia Rashad**
65. b **Writer and poet**
66. c **Alex Haley**
67. a **Amiri Baraka**
68. b **Frederick Douglass**
69. a ***I Know Why the Caged Bird Sings***
70. a **Alice Walker**
71. a ***Beloved***
72. a **Zora Neale Hurston**
73. b **Juanita Hall**
74. c **Diahann Carroll**
75. a **Diana Ross**
76. **False - Diana Ross**
77. c **Actor**
78. b **Edmonia Lewis**
79. a **Missouri**
80. c **Loss of left leg**
81. a **Harriet Beecher Stowe**
82. b **19**
83. **True**
84. b ***Driving Miss Daisy***
85. a **Billy Strayhorn**
86. b **Black Swan**

87. a Artistic paintings
88. b Malcolm Jamal Warner
89. c Musician
90. a Herb and Jamaal
91. b 1989
92. c Jump Start
93. a Boyz II Men
94. b Gregory Hines
95. c Terry McMillan
96. a Vanessa Williams
97. b Whitney Houston
98. c Curtis
99. a Luther
100. b M.C. Hammer
101. c "Star Trek"
102. a Morrie Turner
103. b Naomi Campbell
104. c Arthur Mitchell
105. a Mal Goode
106. b Richard Lawson
107. c Katherine Dunham
108. a Whoopi Goldberg
109. b "Solid Gold"
110. c Don Cornelius
111. a William Wells Brown
112. a *My Bondage & My Freedom*
113. b W. C. Handy
114. c Robin Givens
115. c Washington, D.C.
116. b New Orleans
117. c *The House Behind the Cedars*
118. a 1920s
119. True
120. True
121. b *Native Son*
122. c Bebop
123. a Dizzy Gillespie
124. b Dizzy Gillespie
125. c Dizzy Gillespie
126. a Paul Laurence Dunbar
127. b Denzel Washington
128. c *Clotel; or, the President's Daughter*
129. True
130. a *Georgia, Georgia*
131. b Motown
132. c $3.40
133. a Motown
134. b Detroit
135. c Benjamin Hanby

136. a **Lorraine Hansberry**
137. b **Gwendolyn Brooks**
138. c ***Annie Allen***
139. a **Nat "King" Cole**
140. b **"The Nat King Cole Show"**
141. c **A hair tonic company**
142. c **Weatherman**
143. a ***The Fire Next Time***
144. b **Marian Anderson**
145. b **Godfrey Cambridge**
146. a **Al Jarreau**
147. b **John H. Johnson**
148. b ***A Raisin in the Sun***
149. b **Oprah Winfrey**
150. b **Eddie Murphy**
151. b ***Cry Freedom***
152. b **Bill Cosby**
153. b **Beverly Johnson**
154. b **John Elroy Sanford**
155. a **Richard Pennington**
156. b **Robert Scott Duncanson**
157.　 **False - Richard Pryor**
158. a **Bird**
159. a **Ida B. Wells-Barnett**
160. a **Julian Abele**
161. a **Bean**
162. b **Joseph Oliver**
163. a **Cicely Tyson**
164.　 **True**
165. a **Stanley Kirk Burrell**
166. a **Forest Whitaker**
167. a **Mother of the Blues**
168. a **Florence Price**
169. b **Arthur Mitchell**
170. a **Frances Ellen Watkins Harper**
171. b **Dean Dixon**
172. a **Kadeem Hardison**
173. a **Billy Eckstine**
174. a **1983**
175. a **Michael Jackson**
176. a **Marian Anderson**
177.　 **False - Scott Joplin**
178. a **Count Basie**
179. a **Toni Morrison**
180. a **Scott Joplin**
181. b **"Every Beat of My Heart"**
182. a **Ahmad Jamal**
183. b **Negro Ensemble Company**
184. a **Stepin Fetchit**

185. b Erroll Garner
186. b Aaron Douglas
187. c Diana Sands
188. a David Walker
189. a Lois Jones Pierre-Noel
190. b Man of Sorrow
191. a Marilyn McCoo
192. b Isaac Hayes
193. a Langston Hughes
194. a Edward Kennedy Ellington
195. b 1959
196. b Dinah Washington
197. a Bill "Bojangles" Robinson
198.   True
199. b Bill Robinson
200. b Joe Oliver
201. b Billy Taylor
202. c Sousa
203. b Flip Wilson
204. a Dionne Warwick
205. c Clarence Clemons
206. c Earl Graves
207.   True
208.   True
209.   False - He founded Motown Record Corporation
210. a "The Twist"
211. b 33
212. c Joshua Johnston
213. c *Ragtime*
214. c Maya Angelou
215. c Teacher
216. b Actor
217. c James Edwards
218. a Singer
219. a Black writers and artists
220. a Whitney Museum
221. a *Thriller*
222. b Frederick Eversley
223. c "All My Children"
224. a An opera singer
225. a Rufus Thomas
226. c Piano
227. a Isaiah Jackson
228. c Katherine Dunham
229. a William Wells Brown
230. c Saxophone
231. a Max Robinson
232. b Joseph Douglass
233. a Sculptress

234. c  **Nipsey Russell**
235. c  **Paul Robeson**
236. b  **Jazz**
237. a  **Nightclub**
238. c  **1990**
239.    **False - "The Godfather of Soul"**
240.    **False - The film was *Rhapsody in Blue***
241. c  **Philadelphia Museum of Art**
242. a  **Eddie Murphy**
243. b  **Deacon**
244. b  **Ballads**
245. b  **Painter**
246. c  **Bessie Smith**
247. c  **Jackson**
248.    **True**
249. b  **Cleopatra**
250. c  **Count Basie's**
251. c  **Richard Pryor**
252. a  **Richard Wright**
253. b  **Authentic record of lynchings**
254. c  **Oklahoma City, Oklahoma**
255. a  **Ralph Ellison**
256. a  **Alex Haley**
257. b  **Characterized plight of slaves**
258. c  **Westerns**
259. b  **Paul Laurence Dunbar**
260. b  **Countee Cullen**
261. c  ***Blues People***
262. a  **African American music**
263. c  **Phillis Wheatley**
264.    **False - Lerone Bennett, Jr., wrote the book**
265. a  **Horace Clayton**
266. b  **1906**
267. a  **Singer with a range of 27 octaves**
268. b  **Nina Mae McKinney**
269. c  **Drum**
270. b  **Xylophone**
271. c  **Philadelphia Concert Orchestra**
272. b  **Scott Joplin**
273. c  **"Jelly Roll Blues"**
274. c  **A fiddle-playing cowboy**
275. b  **Muddy Waters**
276. c  **Stevie Wonder**
277. c  **Lisa Bonet**
278. c  **Michael Jackson**
279. b  **Henry Tanner**
280. a  **Justin Holland**
281. b  **Bessie Smith**
282. a  **Award-winning music compositions**

283. b  Anta Cheikh Diop
284. b  Chancellor Williams
285. b  Louis Gossett, Jr.
286. c  Benjamin E. Mays
287. c  Lerone Bennett, Jr.
288. b  *The Black Abolitionists*
289. b  *The Lost Zoo*
290. a  Black music
291. c  Joseph "King" Oliver
292. c  Jelly Roll
293. c  "Mission Impossible"
294. c  *In Cold Blood*
295. a  Pop-Gospel
296. b  Musical bow
297. c  En Vogue
298.    True
299. b  Luther Vandross
300. a  Lawrence Tayrue
301. c  "Benson"
302. c  Sherman Hemsley
303. a  Toni Morrison
304. a  "The Jeffersons" and "Amen"
305. c  "60 Minutes"
306. b  T. C.
307. a  Gary Coleman
308. b  "The Little Rascals"
309. c  Eddie "Rochester" Anderson
310. b  Duke Ellington
311.    False - Gwendolyn Brooks
312. a  Gwendolyn Brooks
313.    True
314. c  Romare Bearden
315. a  Billy Strayhorn
316.    True
317. c  James Baldwin
318. b  Frances Harper
319. a  Cicely Tyson
320. c  James Baskett
321.    True
322. c  *No Way Out*
323. c  Maya Angelou
324. c  Spike Lee
325. b  Whitney Houston

# INDEX

63